Brass

Wendy Lynch

Heinemann

Schools Library and Information Services

www.heinemann.co.uk/library
Visit our website to find out more information about **Heinemann Library** books.

To order:
☎ Phone ++44 (0)1865 888066
🖷 Send a fax to ++44 (0)1865 314091
🖳 Visit the Heinemann Bookshop at www.heinemann.co.uk/library to browse our catalogue
and order online.

First published in Great Britain by Heinemann Library, Halley Court, Jordan Hill, Oxford
OX2 8EJ, a division of Reed Educational and Professional Publishing Ltd. Heinemann
is a registered trademark of Reed Educational & Professional Publishing Ltd.

OXFORD MELBOURNE AUCKLAND JOHANNESBURG BLANTYRE
GABORONE IBADAN PORTSMOUTH NH (USA) CHICAGO

Designed by Visual Image
Illustration by Jane Watkins
Originated by Dot Gradations
Printed in China

ISBN 0 431 12900 2 (hardback)   ISBN 0 431 12906 1 (paperback)

06 05 04 03 02   06 05 04 03 02
10 9 8 7 6 5 4 3 2   10 9 8 7 6 5 4 3 2 1

British Library Cataloguing in Publication Data

Lynch, Wendy
Brass instruments – Juvenile literature
I. Title
788.9

Acknowledgements
The Publishers would like to thank the following for permission to reproduce photographs: Corbis pp14, 20, 22, 24,
Gareth Boden pp28, 29, Photodisc pp6, 7, 10, Photofusion pp8 (Richard Alton), 9 (Ray Roberts), Pictor pp4, 19, 23,
Powerstock (Zefa) p21, Redferns pp11 (Odile Noel), 15 (Odile Noel), 16 (Odile Noel), 27 (Paul Massey), Rex p25,
Robert Harding p17, Stone pp5, 26, The Stock Market p12, Travel Ink (Derek Allan) p18.

Cover photograph reproduced with permission of Photodisc.

Every effort has been made to contact copyright holders of any material reproduced in this book.
Any omissions will be rectified in subsequent printings if notice is given to the Publisher.

Any words appearing in the text in bold, **like this**, are explained in the Glossary.

Contents

Making music together

There are many musical instruments in the world. Each instrument makes a different sound. We can make music together by playing these instruments in a band or an **orchestra**.

Bands and orchestras are made up
of different groups of instruments.
One of these groups is called brass.
You can see brass instruments in this
brass band.

What are brass instruments?

Brass instruments are often made of brass. Brass is a strong metal and it does not **rust**. These instruments can also be made of other metals. Some are even made of wood, horn or shell.

trumpet

tuba

To make a sound with brass instruments, you press your lips against the **mouthpiece** and blow air into them. When you play brass instruments, the movement of your lips helps to make the sound.

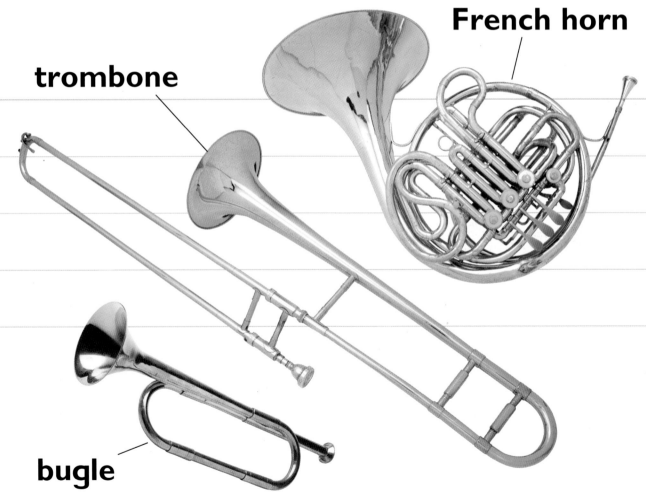

French horn

trombone

bugle

The trumpet

The trumpet is a brass instrument. It is often played in school today. You can play the trumpet alone. This is called playing **solo**. You can learn to play the trumpet with a teacher.

You can play the trumpet with other instruments, like a trombone. You can play in a group, a brass band or an **orchestra**.

Making a noise

The trumpet is a long, thin, **coiled** metal tube. It has a **mouthpiece** at one end and a bell at the other. On top of the tube are three small buttons called valves.

bell

valves

mouthpiece

When you blow into the trumpet it makes the air inside the tube move quickly from side to side. This movement is called **vibration**. When air vibrates, it makes a sound.

Changing the sound

To play the trumpet, you blow into the **mouthpiece**. You also press the valves with your fingers to change the sound. A sound can be high or low. This is called **pitch**.

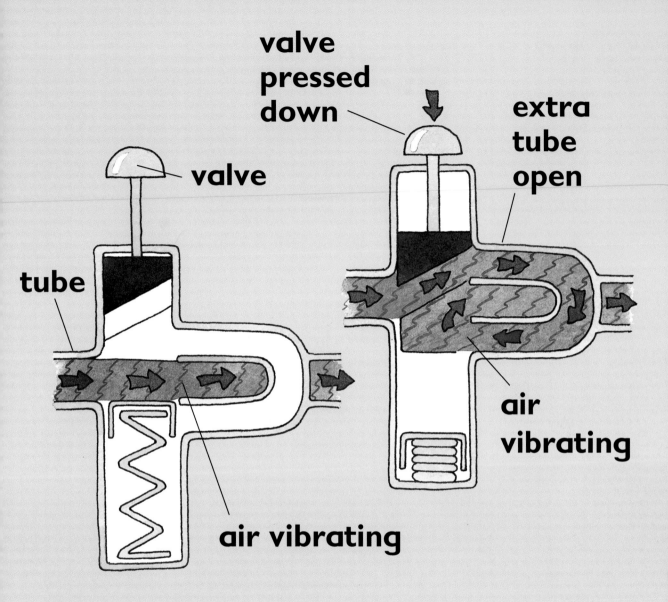

valve
pressed
down

valve

extra
tube
open

tube

air
vibrating

air vibrating

If you press the valves, you open
another part of the tube. This makes
the sound lower because the air
vibrates more slowly.

The cornet and the trombone

The cornet is like a trumpet but smaller. You can sometimes hear the cornet playing **solo** in a brass band. It has a sweet sound. You can also hear the cornet in **jazz** music.

You play the trombone in a different way from other brass instruments. The trombone has a slide. The player moves the slide in and out to change the notes.

Big brass

The tuba is a large brass instrument with a rich, low sound. It takes a lot of breath to play the tuba because it is so big. To play the tuba, you sit down with the instrument on your knee.

The sousaphone is usually played standing up. The player must stand inside the tube of the instrument.

Marching band

In a marching band, you can hear brass, and other instruments. All the players play their musical instruments as they move. They read music from cards clipped onto the instrument.

Marching bands often lead parades through towns or cities on special days of celebration. Brass instruments can be heard from a long way away.

The wider family

The bugle is a small copper horn. You can only play a few notes on the bugle. The bugle has been used by armies for hundreds of years, to send signals to soldiers.

The conch trumpet is made from a shell. It is a brass instrument because you play it by buzzing your lips into the **mouthpiece**. You can hear the conch trumpet from a long distance.

Around the world

You can find brass instruments all over the world. The dung chen comes from Tibet. You can hear this trumpet in a **Buddhist temple**.

The didgeridoo comes from the branch of a tree in Australia. Insects eat the wood inside the branch until it is **hollow**. The **Aborigines** paint the wood. It is then ready to play.

Famous musicians and composers

People have played the trumpet for hundreds of years. A famous **composer** called Haydn wrote a trumpet **concerto**.

You can also hear the cornet, trumpet and trombone in **jazz** and **blues** music. Wynton Marsalis is a famous trumpet player.

New music

Today you can also hear brass instruments in **soul**, **rock** and **pop bands**. This band is playing soul music. When you listen to soul music, it is easy to hear the brass instruments.

A **synthesizer** is a keyboard which can **imitate** many different sounds. You can make the sounds of all the brass instruments using a synthesizer.

Sound activity

You can feel what it is like to play a brass instrument. Close your lips together tightly. Now blow against your fingers until you make a noise. Can you feel your lips **vibrating**?

Roll a sheet of A4 paper into the shape of a cone. Buzz your lips into the small end. You can make a different sound by placing your hand against the large end of the cone as you blow.

Thinking about brass

You can find the answers to all of these questions in this book.

1. Why is brass good for making musical instruments?

2. What is a valve on a brass instrument for?

3. Which brass instrument do you need to stand inside to play?

4. Where can you hear a dung chen?

Glossary

Aborigines people who first lived in Australia

blues old style of slow, sad music from America

Buddhist temple special building where people who believe in Buddhism go to pray

coiled something curled or wound into a ring

composer person who writes new music

concerto piece of music in three parts, often for one instrument and an orchestra You say *con-cher-toe*

hollow empty inside

imitate copy

jazz old style of music from America that is often made up as it is played

mouthpiece part of the instrument placed in or near the mouth

orchestra large group of musicians who play their musical instruments together You say *or-kes-tra*

pitch the highness or lowness of a sound or musical note

pop bands group of musicians who play music of the last fifty years. A lot of people like this music.

rock bands group of musicians who play a kind of pop music with a strong beat

rust brown or red coating that forms on some metals when they get wet

solo song or piece of music for one person

soul bands group of musicians who play a kind of pop music that is full of feeling. Brass instruments are often played by soul bands.

synthesizer electronic instrument that can make or change many different sounds You say *sintha-size-a*

vibrate move up and down or from side to side very quickly

Index